# 12 Winning Leadership Qualities

## Unleash The Leader Instinct Within You!

**from the library of the**
**New Thrive Learning Institute**

Get Related Materials

from Our Free Library

**Instant Access – Join Here**

*Click or type into your browser:*

*http://livesensical.com/go/byob/*

## LEGAL NOTICE

# Table of Contents

## *INTRODUCTION*

You have what it takes. You know you are the most suited person for the job. You're so positive that you can lead a lot of people towards good business...Or so you think. Because if you really are, then why did John, from the other department, got the job you've been dying to have since you entered the company?

Leadership is more than just being confident that you can manage a number of people and make them follow your lead. Each one of us influences at least ten thousand other people during our lifetime. Hence, the question is not whether we can influence these people, but in what manner shall we influence them.

There are instances that competitors suddenly give up believing that they just can never be leaders. Maybe I'm not really born to lead, they think. On the contrary, the key to effective leadership does not depend primarily in the abilities we are born with, but in techniques, skills, character, and qualities that we are open to develop throughout life.

Leadership does not come out merely from the inner personality of the individual or from his philosophy of leadership, but from his enthusiasm to become the person other people will follow. This means that how a leader reacts when his power or safety is challenged, and how he interprets the world around him, is crucial to developing strong and effective leadership qualities.

It is true that there is always room for improvement for every one of us. David Rooke, partner at Harthill Consulting and co-author of the Harvard Business Review article Leadership Can Be Learnt, said that there is room for us all to develop and maximize our leadership capabilities.

"The lessons for businesses to learn lie in their willingness to make leadership development a central pillar in the way they operate and a powerful force for transforming their fortunes," he said.

So to future leaders of the world, worry no more. This report is designed to help you develop the winning leadership qualities you have been lacking of and increase your personal and organizational success. Whether your desire is to lead a student campaign, start a business, or reach the top of the world, the first step in achieving it is to know what it takes to be a leader...and a winner in one.

So, let's start bringing out the leader in you!

## WINNING QUALITY # 1: A Leader Should Have a Vision and Be Able to Cast It.

Vision is the primary and most important quality for a leader to possess. It is what leads and motivates him towards success - the fire that lights the road he will be traveling so he will not get lost along the journey. It is the sense of direction that draws him forward. A leader without a vision is like a traveler who has no direction as to where he is going.

Jeff Earlywine, a famous author, compares casting vision with fishing. He had made such comparison because that hobby of his was one of his greatest loves as a kid. That love, according to him, developed quickly because his family owned a little bait shop that was located near Toledo Bend Lake in Louisiana. Toledo Bend is known for its large bass and large quantity of crappies.

He soon found out that there is a lot more to fishing than just catching fish. Learning to cast a fishing lure into a tree-covered fish hole takes great skill. However, casting is just the start; you have to learn to make the lure look irresistible to the fish below, so irresistible that an attack is inevitable.

Casting a vision for your organization works much the same way – the vision should be effective, useful, and doable so that success would be easy to catch. It is the starting process that when done well would lead to a flourishing realization.

Therefore, to be a leader, you must have a vision. This vision is the same direction as yours that your people will walk through, having you to lead the way for them. Without a clear vision of what you want to do and where you want to go, you just cannot hope for anything to happen.

Bringing Out that Vision in You

To develop a vision, look within yourself. Vision comes from the inner self. Hence, you cannot say that it is difficult or you just cannot make one. Every one has his mold and personality where he can extract a vision for himself and for his people.

Vision does not come suddenly like some magical tricks, as some people seem to believe. It grows from the leader's past experiences and history of the people around him. Draw on your talents, dreams, and desires. Look to your calling if you have one.

When you finally have that vision that is indispensable to your leadership, don't just end there. Cast it...effectively. This is where your leadership begins.

Casting your vision to your people involves five steps:

**1.       Listen.**  Since vision starts within, you have to listen and feel what your mind and heart really want. What stirs your heart? What is your greatest desire? What do you dream about? If what you wish to pursue does not really come from the inner depths of you, it would be difficult, if not impossible, to achieve it.

On the other hand, in fulfilling a greater vision, you need a good team to support you. Nobody can accomplish big things alone. Hence, listen to good advice from a person who has more experiences than you do in leadership. Find a mentor. Seek for help occasionally. Nothing is wrong in asking for guidance. Even leaders need to be taught to learn.

Lastly, you should not be confined within your limited capabilities. A truly valuable vision must be coupled with faith.

**2.       Prepare your mind.** The process of casting a vision begins with you, the leader. As mentioned earlier, the vision of your organization begins in your mind and heart. It is something that you can feel, taste, see, hear, and touch with your soul. Your vision should be greater than your past memories, mistakes, and accomplishments. If you have a vision in mind, you will know what to aim for and will never get lost along the journey. Dissatisfaction and discouragement are not caused by the absence of practice, but by the absence of vision. Warren Bennis, author of The Leadership Institute, even said, "Leadership is the capacity to translate vision into reality."

The best way for your vision to become clear in your mind and heart is to retreat to a quiet and tranquil place – somewhere that will allow your mind to think creatively and crystallize the vision.

**3.     Ask questions.** Introduce your people to thought provoking questions that will help them see the vision and dream in your heart, and begin acquiring that vision, too. Your questions may be like:

> - What is one thing that our staff needs to do their job better?

> - What actions need to be taken in order to increase our sales and/or income?

> - What changes need to be made in order to guarantee we accomplish our objectives?

**4.     Identify the problem.** During this step, discuss with your team the challenges keeping the questions you have arrived at from being answered and acted upon - challenges such as why sales are not reaching predetermined goals, why customers are not returning, or why families are suffering just as much within the church walls as they are outside the church. Being aware of what the problem really is will lead to knowing what necessary steps have to be taken. Overcoming these challenges will put the organization on the pathway to accomplishing its objectives and your vision.

**5.     Proceed to a solution.** The last step in this process is to determine the solution to the above challenges. This is the where you share your heart's vision and get the opinions of your leadership team. Everyone must be convinced that the solution will help your organization accomplish your vision. It is very important at this point to remember K.I.S.S. – Keep It Short & Simple.

## WINNING QUALITY # 2: A Leader Should Be Willing to Take Responsibilities.

Who would forget the ever-famous line of Peter Parker's grandfather, "With great power comes great responsibility." The society expects Spiderman, a comic book, TV, and movie superhero, to be responsible for saving his town, or even the world, in some instances, from evil because he has super powers. From all the episodes he appeared in, he never let us down. With the power he possesses, he makes sure to be responsible in using it for the good of the people around him.

Leadership is not at all different from being superheroes. Yes, you may not have super powers like Superman and Spiderman, but you have the authority to lead other people towards success. This is so much greater and stronger since it is a power that can be used by real people in this real world.

Hence, being a leader requires great sense of responsibility, the second quality a successful leader should attain. The power to lead your people towards aiming your vision comes with responsibilities like making sure they are on the right direction, being aware of each and everyone's tasks and mistakes, and putting them back on the right track when they get lost.

Who said it is easy to be a leader? Well, it is not...It comes with tons of responsibilities. True leaders are willing to accept them all.

There are instances where sometimes it makes us feel better to blame somebody or something else when something goes wrong in a task. However, this should not be practiced, especially by a good leader!

A leader should take full responsibility of a task - not just before he accepts to take it, but also after it has been accomplished. As much as he is responsible for his team's success, he should also be responsible for any failure. He represents the whole team so whatever happens to it, he is the one responsible.

Making excuses and blaming something or someone else for failed jobs is not a quality of a good leader. What he should do, instead, is to accept the fact that something went wrong with the organization, even if it is not his fault. It is normal to make mistakes. In fact, mistakes are opportunities to learn something better. As a leader, he must ensure that the team members learn from these mistakes and that these errors will not be repeated next time.

You may not have full control over other people and are not expected to have full control over their actions, but you have full control of your own reactions. Knowing what to do over unexpected and unpredictable situations will make you responsible, hence giving you the feeling of power.

## Bringing Out the More Responsible You

Sometimes, we never get leadership and trust from people more authoritative than us – because, according to them, we are just not "responsible enough." What is the measure of being "responsible enough"? Below is a list of steps on how to draw responsibility out of our shells:

1.      **Develop self-awareness.** As a leader, you should know your own strengths and weaknesses to be able to view your behavior objectively. Also, recognize your shortcomings, open yourself to feedback, and make changes when necessary. When you are aware of yourself and your personality as a whole, you will know what tasks you should engage in and what situations you feel you are not capable of handling.

Dr. Gerald Bell, business consultant and professor at the University of North Carolina, Chapel Hill, N.C, advises us on how to expand our self-knowledge, "Study yourself closely and practice self-assessment techniques to learn how you behave and the effects you have on others. Ask others for their opinions or criticisms and what you can do to become a better leader."

**2.     Do not equate responsibility with worry.** When we hear the word responsibility, we often think to ourselves, "another task, another problem!" However, responsibility is more than worrying about things given to us to work out. Consider this short story:

One night at the end of the second shift, an employee walked out of the plant and passed the porter. As head of operations, he had started his day at the beginning of the first shift. The porter said, "Mr. Smith, I sure wish I had your pay, but I don't want your worry."

The porter equated responsibility and worry. Perhaps he does not want to carry the office work home like what he does as a porter. This is not reasonable, especially if you want to become an effective leader.

Say, the vice-president of a prestigious company and the porter are paid the same money, who would you want to be? Carrying responsibility should not intimidate you, because the joy of accomplishment – the feeling of helping other people – is what leadership is all about.

**3.     Take risks.** Effective leaders have the courage to act in situations where results and success are uncertain. They are willing to risk failure. In doing this, you always have to be prepared. Analyze the situation and your options. List the pros and the cons for each option you have, and then assign each choice a risk factor rating from 1 to 5. Next, determine the likelihood that each outcome will occur. This will help you know how much risk you are willing to take.

Also, do not expect perfection. No one is perfect. In fact, leaders grow by making mistakes.

**4.     Be ready to admit your mistakes.** Everyone makes mistakes. It is normal. Avoid making excuses and blaming others for something you did wrong. Admitting your mistakes and failures will even make people respect you more, as you are true to yourself.

## *WINNING QUALITY # 3: A Leader Should Have Strength of Character.*

According to John C. Maxwell, author of Leadership 101 and Developing the Leaders around You, the first thing to look for in any kind of leader or potential leader is strength of character. "I have found nothing more important than this quality," he said.

First, we need to define character. D. L. Moody said, "Character is what you are in the dark." What Moody meant by this is that character is what you really are when no one is looking, not the cover-up that you allow others to see. Character is what guides your actions and produces the words you speak. Character is your unique identity, your personality, the sum total of your individual characteristics.

Character can be good or bad. Strength of character refers to the strong and good character. A person strong in character is someone who stands for what is right, who has the "backbone" to express and live out his convictions.

What are the qualities that make up good character? These include honesty, integrity, devotion, self-discipline, determination, dependability, perseverance, conscientiousness, patience, and a strong work ethic. A person with right character does what he says, and says what he does. His reputation is solid. He respects himself, his family, and his nation.

As there is no perfect person in the world, all of us lack a few strong qualities mentioned above. It should not be ignored for, according to Maxwell, serious character flaws will eventually make a leader ineffective – every time.

Hence, if you notice any of the following characteristics and behaviors below, you might be losing your potential to be an effective leader:

   - not being able to do the tasks given to you

- undone obligations and broken promises

- not taking responsibility for your actions

- failure to meet deadlines and making tons of excuses

- being oversensitive to criticisms and comments

Start taking control of your actions and develop the right strength of character. Although character flaws cannot be changed overnight, it can be changed through right practice and attitude.

## Bringing Out that Strong Character in You

You don't want to be the weak link that will disentangle the chain that binds your team, do you? Being the leader, you should be the one with the strong character that your people would imitate. Be their role model and show them who the real boss is!

1.      **Believe in yourself.** Before you expect anybody else to believe in you, you should be the first person to believe in who you are and in what you can do. Look at and see yourself the way you want others to see you. If you want others to respect you, learn to respect yourself. If you want others to love you, love yourself first. Focus on the things you do well and try to develop those you are not good at.

2.      **Engage in training.** Practice makes perfect. Even if you think it is helpless for you to possess a quality you never really have, by constantly engaging yourself in situations necessary to observe such quality, you will eventually realize that you are slowly achieving it. For instance, if you know you lack patience (but since patience is needed to strengthen your character and you need to develop it), exercise it by falling in long lines, waiting to be served in restaurants, etc.

3.      **Develop mental toughness.** No one can lead without getting criticisms or without facing discouragement from other people. A potential leader needs mental toughness for such threatening situations. A tough-minded

leader sees things as they are and knows how to adjust when needed. Ask authorized persons to criticize your work constantly. Treat criticisms as constructive, and learn from mistakes. Never be oversensitive.

**4.      Follow right examples.** Even leaders need a model. Get to know people with strong qualities. Make friends and blend with them. When you have chosen a person who possesses something you always wanted to have, you will emulate what he is doing in order to be like him.

**5.      Display integrity.** Leaders must possess qualities such as honesty, uprightness, and trustworthiness before others will follow them. Warren Bennis says qualities that establish trust are competence, constancy, caring, candor, and congruity, which he defines as authenticity, reliability, and feeling comfortable with oneself.

To learn to assess your integrity, actively seek feedback from other people, whether they are friends, co-workers, and even employees, to determine your work attitude. Know whether your values and sense of responsibility coincide with expectations from you.

## *WINNING QUALITY # 4: A Leader Should Have Effective Communication Skills.*

Communication is the key to understanding any issue between two or more parties. An efficient leader must never stand in front of his people without the skill of effective communication.

President Gerald Ford once said, "Nothing in life is more important than the ability to communicate effectively." This is because without the ability to communicate, a leader cannot effectively cast his vision and call his people to act on that vision. Just imagine how a group of people could make a decision if their leader cannot even direct the flow of conversations.

In many ways, effective communication begins with mutual respect. It should bring out inspirations, encouragement, or instructions for others to do their best. When you respect people, you will never appear rude to them. Consequently, by treating them with respect, you get cooperation, enthusiastically given instead of forcefully given. Respected individuals are going to work harder to become peak performers, wanting to do more and more.

If people like you, they will work harder for you. Otherwise, they might be working just to keep their jobs, but not really giving their best efforts. People might perform to keep their jobs because duty and responsibility demand that they do a job well. However, love and encouragement enable people to do work remarkably. When you communicate to people that you genuinely like and respect them, and follow that up with consistency of action, you establish rapport with and confidence in your people that will make a difference.

Communication is not necessarily an easy skill to learn, but it really begins with seriously listening to what other people say. By listening with respect, you will learn things that can make a difference. Consistency will be the result, and consistent performance is the key to excellence.

## Bringing Out the Effective Communicator in You

Effective communication is not about what we want to say, but what we want the people around us to understand about the things we say. In The 100 Simple Secrets of Successful People by David Niven, Ph.D, the success secret of Newsman David Brinkley is revealed. He credits a teacher's simple advice for much of his success, "He said to me, 'The faster you speak, the less people will understand you. Take that to heart,' And I did."

Besides speaking slowly, which we got from the excerpt above, here are other ways to develop effective communication skills:

1.      **Discuss, don't argue.** The purpose of having conversations between you and other people is to exchange views and information, and to know what they think about certain topics. A good leader explains calmly what he believes in and never gets affected by any tension that might arise.

2.      **Focus on the speaker.** Those who tend to focus mainly on themselves and their own opinions are not effective communicators. To be a good communicator, focus on the response of the people you are talking to. Read both their verbal and non-verbal signs.

3.      **Learn to listen.** A successful communication model tells us that when communicator 1 speaks, communicator 2 listens (and vice versa). This way, all messages are received and understood. Allow others to speak their minds. During this time, what you ought to do is listen to what they have to say.

4.      **Develop eye contact while communicating.** Making eye contact to the people you are talking to or people talking to you displays integrity and conviction. Tell them

through such gesture that you are interested and willing to continue the conversation.

**5.** **Never forget to smile.** They say that it takes 47 muscles to frown, but only 17 to smile. Besides spending lesser effort on such gesture, smiling is a sign of opening the lines of communication and welcoming other people to join the conversation. Maxwell reminds, "A smile overcomes innumerable communication barriers, crossing the boundaries of culture, race, age, class, gender, education, and economic status.

## WINNING QUALITY # 5: A Leader Should Have a Positive Attitude.

Tell me a leader who rejects every suggestion his team gives because he is afraid they cannot make it and I will tell you someone who is not fit to be a leader.

Let me quote John Maxwell on how he views positive attitude. In his book, Developing the Leaders around You, he says, "A positive attitude is one of the most valuables assets a person can have in life." It can help you achieve things that may seem impossible to happen.

As a leader, you will need more than a miracle to make certain things happen. As long as you have the right attitude of looking at things, and on how they have to be done, you can eliminate the miracle wishing part.

Most of the time, we become discouraged by how difficult the problems we face are. What we do not know is that it is not really the problems that are difficult to deal with but our attitude towards them. Yes, they may be tough at times and may take a lot of time to solve, but as long as we view them as obstacles that will hinder our way towards our goal, we can never really arrive at the right solution.

Why don't we see these problems as challenges...as something to spice our journey up? Not all roads to success are smooth. Often, there are bumps and humps. If we miss our turn, we might get lost and end up starting all over again.

See the big picture. Look beyond the problem. A positive leader will not dwell on a difficult situation and be discouraged by it, but will believe that he can and he ought to surpass it in order to reach his goals. With positive attitude, he never accepts defeat. Instead, he fights the noble battle until the very end.

Believing that you can make something happen is not at all a small thing when you put faith in yourself and believe that you can do it. What the mind says, the body will follow. It is a chain reaction.

When people see that their leader believes and strives hard for accomplishing a task, they will do the same. Imagine, if a single believer can make something happen, then how much more things can a team of believers bring out?

## Bringing Out the Positive Person in You

Ok, so you always see the glass half-empty. But you know what? Even if half of the water spills on the floor, it still contains water...and it is half full! Now how can you still see the good things in everything...even if you are pessimistic all the time? The answers lie below.

**1.     Keep your mind focused on important things.** Set goals and priorities for what you think and do. Visualize practicing your actions and the results you expect from them. Develop an effective strategy for dealing with problems. Concentrate on things that need to be taken seriously; but at the same time, take time to relax and enjoy.

**2.     Keep a list of your goals and actions.** Familiarize yourself with things you want to accomplish and with the ways you must undertake to complete them. When you are aware of these things, your body will immediately carry out the actions you need to execute in making these things happen.

**3.     Be detached from the outcome.** Life is often compared to a Ferris wheel, or a ball, or anything that is round, because of the fact that sometimes we are on the top, and sometimes at the bottom. This only means that there will be times in our lives when some things would not turn out according to what we want them to be. Nevertheless, face them. Do not be annoyed if you do not get what you desire. Do not be discouraged. Do not become too attached to the probable results, but just do your best in everything.

**4.    Balance your desires.** We live in a place of opposites and differences – happiness and sadness, pleasure and pain, tears and laughter, love and hate. This is how the cycle of life goes. We can never have all the good things in life at the same time. In wealth, there will always be people who will not be fortunate enough. Measure and moderation is the primary key.

**5.    Be realistic.** Make sure that what you want is something possible. Hoping for something to happen, which would never really materialize in real life, will only bring you disappointment. Success cannot be gained overnight...but it can be gained no matter what. Believe and have faith.

**6.    Associate with positive people.** In classrooms, work places, or simply anywhere you go where there are groups of people, look for optimistic ones. Associate, hang out, and discuss matters with them. They can help you build self-confidence and self-esteem.

**7.    Ask questions.** Asking or seeking for guidance can bring no harm. It does not equate to dumbness and ignorance; rather, it is associated with seeking more information and understanding matters clearly, which is good for you as a leader since you need to learn more things in guiding your people. Remember, with more knowledge, there is also more power.

**8.    Count your blessings.** Focus on what you have rather than what you don't have. Positive outcomes emerge when we know we are abundant of this life's blessings. On the other hand, absence of desires will only bring discontentment and disappointment that will only waste our time. So be thankful and appreciative of all the blessings that life has to offer.

**9.    Kiss your worries goodbye.** At the end of everyday, before going to sleep, there is no need to keep bad experiences and unhappy moments that had happened during the day. Let them go, throw them out of the window, and kiss them goodbye. Dream sweetly. As a new day unfolds, new hope arises. Keep believing.

## WINNING QUALITY # 6: A Leader Should Be Influential.

The job of a true leader is to lead his people towards a certain successful goal. He simply cannot do this if he has no influence over them. Without influence, he cannot make other people do what he wants them to do.

An ordinary child can influence his parents to buy him a new toy. His parents, on the other hand, can influence their child to do his assignments first before playing. Students can influence their teachers to move their exam on the 5th, instead of on the 1st of the month. Your neighbor can influence you to buy a certain brand of bath soap instead of the one you are using. In other words, anybody can influence other people, may it be kids, students, teachers, parents, your neighbor, or your co-workers. Our society is revolving around influences.

So what makes you excused from being influential when you are the boss, the leader, the one everybody looks up to? In fact, you should be more influential than anybody else should because you are leading people into reaching a common goal. They need your influence!

Most people do their jobs because they need to. They perform in exchange of a salary they can use for everyday living. However, if these people were under a leader who has an effective influence over them, they would do their job because they want to...because they are able to learn from doing it...and because they know that it is for the attainment of the team's goal...without really keeping in mind the pay they would get. People will follow their leader's instructions gladly and confidently, even without any material incentive, if he is influential.

Leadership is not about having the right to stand in front of your people and order them around, but about being the person they will gladly obey even with a casual instruction coming from behind them.

## Bringing Out Mr. Influence in You

As a leader, you should know where your journey ends...
because every follower ought to be behind a leader who
knows where he is going. Otherwise, it is just a waste of time.
If you want to become an influential leader, the following
techniques are essential:

1.      **Assess your people.** A leader should know his
people very well in order to recognize the level of influence
he needs over them. See their potential. Find out their
strengths and weaknesses. Develop what they have and
equip them with things they lack. Factors to look at include
skills and abilities, educational background, knowledge,
dreams and desires, and the likes. By being knowledgeable
about their personality and experiences, you will clearly
understand how to influence each one of them.

2.      **Move them with your words.** A great leader
knows how to communicate with his people effectively. Use
the same thoughts and words that motivate you to do your
best to push them in exerting more effort. Observe even their
non-verbal signals that could help you determine moves that
are more influential.

3.      **Have courage.** A leader must be courageous. He
must be prepared to go where others will not dare. He must
make difficult decisions in the face of opposition and
ridicule, and he must accept, without question, the
responsibility for those decisions. Those who follow look to
their leader to make the decisions. They do not want their
leader hesitant between options. If he is undecided, they will
soon lose faith in him and sense that the whole enterprise is
drifting aimlessly. Neither do they wish to be blamed when
things go wrong. They want someone to lead them, someone
who will take full responsibility for the decisions he makes.

4.      **Develop peer respect.** Peer respect involves
character and personality between you and your people.
Trammell Crow, one of the world's most successful real

estate brokers, said that he looks for people whose associates want them to succeed. He said, "It's tough enough to succeed when everybody wants you to succeed. People who don't want you to succeed are like weights in your running shoes." On the other hand, Maxey Jarmen used to say, "It isn't important that people like you. It's important that they respect you. They may like you but not follow you. If they respect you, they'll follow you, even if perhaps they don't like you."

5.      **Empower.** An effective leader sets clear objectives for his team members, but leaves detailed implementation of these objectives to the discretion and judgment of individual members of the team. As Second World War U.S. General George S. Patton puts it, "Don't tell people how to do things. Tell them what to do and let them surprise you with their results."

6.      **Show enthusiasm and confidence in them.** People want to be motivated. Motivation begins with positive energy and commitment. Your personal ills and corporate pressures are unimportant to your employees. They are concerned about themselves. In good and bad times, you must always express a positive and energetic attitude.

7.      **React and respond.** As you see your people working for you, supply them occasionally with constructive feedbacks on how they are doing. They need to be guided, coached, and taught regularly in order to stay efficient. Talk to them personally one by one. Avoid embarrassing any of them (e.g. telling in front of the team what one member did wrong).

## *WINNING QUALITY # 7: A Leader Should Be Disciplined.*

An effective leader is also a follower. He is the first person he leads. Thus, if he teaches and expects his people to be disciplined, he should be the first one to possess the trait.

In any business and field of work, including our daily routine in the house or with other people, discipline is necessary. Without discipline, we are no more than barbarians who do everything out of instinct without really considering what other people think.

Hence, who would want to listen to an uncontrollable freak? Who would dare follow his instructions out of antagonism and anger? Leaders like you have to acquire the quality of discipline, not only because the society expects you to; but also because in leadership, you will get to meet many people coming from different walks of life. You have to deal with all of them!

You will hear every single story, every single excuse, and every single request that differs from one another. You will see various attitudes – bold, forward, bashful, and unstable. Moreover, by all these, you will get to feel mixed emotions you have never felt before. Thus, in order to prepare yourself for all the things that might arise, you have to have that unremitting discipline to deal with all of them.

As a leader, it is your duty and responsibility to discipline the people you manage. Of course, you cannot do that unless you are one disciplined citizen yourself.

## Bringing Out the Disciplined Individual in You

Being disciplined is more than just controlling your temper or being on time during appointments. It's more on being a whole lot better you...physically, mentally, socially, professionally, and spiritually. Here's how to develop discipline:

1.      **Control your emotions.** Order your mind to project affirmative thoughts especially when fear arises over the outcome of any project. Reverse negative thoughts immediately. Affirmative thoughts constitute controlled emotions.

2.      **Be patient.** Impatience is a sign of immaturity. You should not dig up seeds just to see whether they are growing. Cultivate ideas and desires, execute them, and patiently await the fruits of your labor.

3.      **Work-out a systematic plan for each goal.** Take one task at a time and complete it. You can only move effectively in one direction at one time. You can think only one thought at a time. Discipline yourself to the accomplishment of one task before moving on to the next.

4.      **Expect to pay for what you get.** If you set a high goal, you have to pay a high price. You will have to work, take chances, make sacrifices, and endure setbacks. You will not be able to afford the luxury of laziness or the delights of frequent distraction. When trying to reach for a goal you set, remember that unless you are willing to pay the price, you are just wasting your time.

5.      **Be persistent.** Be ready to lose...temporarily. The greatest leaders in the world became who they are right now because every time they fall and stumble along their journey, they kept standing up and continued moving forward. They kept picking themselves up, returning to the fight long after most men would have given up.

6.      **Stop making excuses!** Even if it's "The timing is just wrong," or "I'm not really qualified," only cowards say such things. They play the if-only game: "If only I had more money (or education)..." or "If only I have the beauty..." The alibis and excuses go on and on; and as long as you really are not committed 100% into something, the list will just not end.

To become a more disciplined person, you have to destroy self-limiting thoughts. As George Bernard Shaw once said, "I don't believe in circumstances. The people who get on in this world are the people who look for the circumstances they want, and if they can't find them, they make them."

## *WINNING QUALITY # 8: A Leader Should Know How to Develop Trust.*

Trust is one of the most important, if not the most important, factors in building any effective relationship among other people. Without trust, a relationship is stagnant and unstable. It will not lead into anything successful.

Warren Bennis and Burt Nanus define trust as "the glue that binds followers and leaders together." Therefore, without trust, there is nobody to lead and there is nobody to follow. A leader would not give his people big responsibilities if he does not trust them. He would not expect good results from them either. On the other hand, his people would hesitate to follow their leader's commands if they do not trust him or any of his decisions.

In simple words, trust should exist between both the leader and his people in order to come up with a sound relationship, which in turn would help them reach their goals. There is nothing to lose when you trust. In fact, you even benefit more from the people you give your trust to, as they exert more effort to match the expectations you assume from them.

On the other side of the story, besides learning to trust your people, you should also be able to build their trust on you. People will not listen to you when they do not trust you. They must believe in you first before they follow your leadership. It is, therefore, the leader's responsibility to develop that trust in him actively from the people around him.

Trust implies accountability (being responsible to other people or things), certainty (being confident and assured), and reliability (being able to depend on due to accuracy). It must be developed every time, but you must be very cautious in handling it. Ever heard the cliché It takes a long period of time to build trust and only seconds to break it?

Beware of actions that can betray trust such as

> - breaking promises (over and over again)

> - telling bad things behind one's back

> - creating untrue stories and gossiping

Remember that trust is the bond that makes the relationship between you (as a leader) and your people last. Build it strongly.

## How to Bring Out the Trustworthy Person in You

1.      **Be yourself.** When you let other people see the real "you," they will not have problems accepting you. Keep yourself away from pretensions. How you see yourself is how people will look at you. Therefore, if you think you are a loser, you should not be surprised when no one respects you. Instead, look at yourself the way you want other people to see you...a leader...a true winner!

2.      **Pursue lifelong learning.** Leaders have a desire to continually learn and grow both personally and socially. They are open to new ideas and continuously seek knowledge that can help them become better. Learn how to expand your knowledge. Maintain a broad focus on things around you. Read a lot, talk to many, share interests with friends. There are many ways on how you can maintain lifelong learning.

3.      **Admit your faults.** Admit it. Nobody is perfect. Everybody commits mistakes, even you, their leader. Do not dwell on them too much. Get over them soon. Do not make excuses. Do not blame others either. People will forgive you for occasional mistakes especially if they can see that you are still learning and growing as a leader. In fact, knowing what your mistakes are and admitting them whole-heartedly is a way of showing courage and another reason for them to trust you.

4.      **Listen.** Good leaders do not just do all the talking. They also listen. Listen to what your people say...and what they don't say. Be sensitive. Anticipate the feelings and needs of your people.

## How to Develop Your Trust in Yourself and in Others

1.      **Forgive and forget.** Mistakes and failures are the root causes of negative thinking. If we somehow learn to let go of all the pain, agony, and fear we try to keep inside our hearts and minds, then there will be nothing more to block our clear thoughts from expressing themselves. Forgive yourself and others for committing mistakes and forget these mistakes.

2.      **Make it a habit to ask questions.** Again, asking does not mean we lack wisdom. Rather, it refers to gathering more information and knowledge from people who are more experienced than we are. Isn't it a blessing to have other people share their insights to us?

3.      **Be open.** We have to accept the fact that we do not know everything. We are continuously learning in every place we go, with every people we meet as everyday passes. We should not close our minds to new ideas and information that comes our way. Our mind is so spacious that it is impossible to fill up completely. Thus, we should accept worthy things that may help us become better and brighter persons.

4.      **Mingle with people on your team.** Have lunch or an after-work drink with them, especially when a staff member has a birthday or there are other reasons to celebrate. You will get to know them better when you get to socialize with them outside of the office. When you know a little more on their personality, you will be able to know what to expect from them.

## *WINNING QUALITY # 9: A Leader Should Be Willing to Make Changes.*

A great leader knows how to break the rules when necessary. Otherwise, he is just merely one of the followers.

Changes are significant, especially when they are put into good use...for the betterment of your organization...farther towards the attainment of your goals. Donna Harrison states, "Great leaders are never satisfied with current levels of performance. They constantly strive for higher and higher levels of achievement."

A great leader sees what is good and what is bad for his team. If something is already sabotaging his plans, whether it is an action, an attitude, or one of his people, he is never afraid to make changes.

Some leaders do not make changes because they try to conform to what is normal. They are afraid to step out of the comfort zone. What they do not know is that there is nothing normal in this life. Everything is created with a little (or big) eccentricity from the others to make it stand out from the crowd, to make it more noticeable or recognizable. That is what makes them ineffective.

Who would want to follow a leader who instructs the same way as the other leader? I mean, if you have to follow somebody else other than the previous leader you know is unproductive, would you go for somebody like him? I won't...because I know he won't do any better.

Be different. Continuously seeking for better and improved ways to do something is not a crime. It is, in fact, genius. It will take you to the top faster. Imagine how long you will be able to reach your goals when you are steady and stagnant for a long period of time. Change for the better.

## Bringing Out the Change-Maker in You

"Positive changes in your life will not be finished today, but it can start today," says David Niven, Ph. D., author of The 100 Simple Secrets of Success.

Here are some techniques on how to handle change properly:

1.    **Be creative.** Whether it's a free lunch from somebody who arrives late in a meeting, or a sing and dance when a simple errand was forgotten, new and fun rules can make everyone's work exciting. Let that mind work and produce imaginative new stuffs. Before you know it, there is no body arriving late any more and all errands are finished on time.

2.    **Take risks.** In every action, there is an equal and opposite reaction. It can be good or bad. So, just take calculated risks. After all, nothing is perfect. Do not expect perfection. No one wins all the time. Leaders grow by learning from the mistakes they made.

3.    **Continue to learn.** A leader does not stop learning. In fact, it is when you become one that you should continue seeking more knowledge. Read newspapers regularly, watch movies and television programs, talk to children, make interviews, visit educational landmarks, and the likes. From new thoughts and ideas you've gathered, develop new policies and decisions for you and your people.

4.    **Say no to the status quo.** John Maxwell describes leaders as "never content with things as they are." To be leading, by definition, according to Maxwell still, is to be in front, breaking new ground, conquering new worlds, moving away from the status quo.

## WINNING QUALITY # 10: A Leader Should Know How and What to Prioritize.

Leadership comes with a great deal of responsibilities. Everything is different from the others in terms of time, the immediate solution to a need, the people involved, decision-making, and a lot more factors. If you are not a good leader, all these thoughts will simply jumble on your mind, making you crazy on what needs to be done first and how it needs to be done.

You do not want to end up in the psycho ward after accomplishing all the tasks given to you, do you? Hey, who said being a leader is a simple job? But why back out? Everything is just a matter of organizing and prioritizing.

Knowing how and what to prioritize will make your life as a leader much simpler and easier. Prioritizing is listing all the things that need to be accomplished in chronological order and doing them one by one from the most to the least important.

Each and every task your team needs to do can be strictly classified in 4 categories:

- important and urgent

- important and not urgent

- not important and urgent

- not important and not urgent

With proper prioritizing, it will be so much easier to identify what needs to be given more focus than others that are not crucial to the team's performance. Effective leadership and management is knowing how to say "NO" to the last 2 categories, while concentrating on the first 2. Restricting yourself from doing unimportant tasks gives you more time in focusing on the important ones.

Another concept every leader should understand is the Pareto Principle or the 80/20 Rule. This simply states that typically 80% of unfocused effort generates only 20% of results. The remaining 80% of results are achieved with only 20% of the effort. Notice how much (or less) effort one can obtain by focusing (or not focusing) on certain tasks?

As a leader, you should be able to identify the things that need to be focused. An organized and systematic leader can make his people follow him without difficulty because they see him as a person with plans and preparations. He knows exactly what needs to be done, and is aware of the direction that they need to walk (or run, in some cases) towards to.

Such quality should not be limited to the leader only. His followers should practice it as well by seeing how their leader does it.

## Bringing Out the Organized and Systematized You

In his book Leadership 101, John Maxwell reminds all leaders, "Remember: It's not how hard you work; it's how smart you work. The ability to juggle three or four high priority projects successfully is a must for every leader." So how can you become a more organized leader?

1.      **Make assessments.** Ask, "Is this the best use of my time right now?" With so many things you ought to do and with very little time, make every moment useful. Analyze every task with the time you have planned to do it. If it is essential and there is nothing more important you can do for that specific time, then go ahead and do it.

2.      **Make a to-do list.** It always helps when you see everything that needs to be accomplished – when there is something to remind you what you need to do during a certain period. In your list, make sure your tasks are listed according to priorities, or you can simply rank them

according to their importance (for example, 5 is the most important task and 1 is the least important task).

**3.    Say NO to things that do not fit your goal.** Every now and then, you would have to encounter many different things, each one with a different level of priority. Those that you know are not about reaching your goals, set them aside. There are far better things to do than concentrate on something that will not really get you anywhere, or that might lead you to a different direction. Be smart. Know how and when to say NO.

**4.    Kick that procrastination habit out of your system.** Instead of saying, "I'll do something else now and finish my work later," you can make it "I'll finish my task now so I can do something else later."

Do you have the wicked unhealthy habit? Here's a secret. Getting rid of procrastination is a just matter of programming the mind. Help yourself by putting thoughts such as "If I didn't get this job done by today, I might lose my job," or "This is far more important than walking my dog / strolling the mall / etc," in mind.

Another trick is to provide yourself a little reward as an incentive. After every important task is finished, treat yourself to a walk in the park or a cone of ice cream. This way, you will realize working can be as much fun as other things you usually do after it.

**5.    Love what you do, do what you love.** It may sound cliché, but it's true. When you love what you are doing, you do not need to force yourself to do it. You know exactly how to accomplish one that really gives you fun and enjoyment...right away.

Do only the things that you love. It would be difficult to perform a task that you hate. If you feel you are not satisfied with how things are going at work, maybe because it is not really for your gratification. Move on. Find your passion.

## WINNING QUALITY # 11: A Leader Should Know What Has to Be Done Next.

Number 76 of David Niven's The 100 Simple Secrets of Successful People is "Always think about what's next."

In that book, there was a story about two people, Barry and Judy Wirth, who own an independent pet store called ProPet. Pet superstore chains soon moved into surrounding towns. These chains had enormous supplies, great varieties, and were able to decrease prices on dog food, the biggest-selling item in the pet store, because of their purchasing power.

The Wirths did not know how to face this challenge of competing with bigger stores, although they have the business expertise to succeed in the pet store business.

"I looked at every aspect of what we did – and looked for things we could do better," Barry explains in The 100 Simple Secrets of Successful People. Although they had been completely independent for a long time, Barry and Judy decided the future lay with a pet supply cooperative that allowed small stores to operate with the collective purchasing capability of hundreds of others.

Barry also mentions in The 100 Simple Secrets of Successful People that the continued success of the store is dependent on one thing: "We need to keep up with the future direction of this business. If you didn't change to keep up, you're going to be blindsided."

Like Barry and Judy, great leaders do not just stop when obstacles block their way, and most especially when those obstacles are cleared out of the way. They continue. Even before any unexpected events happen, they already know what to do next.

The Wirths already knew that they couldn't monopolize the pet store business. They knew that one day, superstores would emerge all over town to be their competitors. They knew how not to give up by knowing exactly what to do when that happens.

Knowing the cause and consequences of each action being taken is an ability that leaders should develop. They should be aware of each option there is in solving a problem and should be able to identify the pros and cons of each one. They should know how to strategize. If we do Plan A, Outcome 1 or 2 could happen. If Outcome 1 happens, we should wait. But if Outcome 2 happens, then we should proceed with Plan B immediately.

A great leader should be able to see the big picture. He should be able to focus on the entire project and not just dwell on petty problems. He concentrates on the present, but considers the future equally. Leadership is not about getting along with your people on this present journey, but leading them towards tomorrow's success.

## Bringing Out the Planner in You

Every great leader has a clear vision. With this vision is an outstanding plan that would lead him and his people in making it happen. The following aspects are crucial in planning.

1.      **Set a little time off.** Walk alone in the park, order coffee while sitting back at a cozy café, or just lay back on your front yard. Whatever it is, set some quiet time for yourself to be able to just think and plan. Sometimes the best ideas come out when you are alone and secluded. Record any of your thoughts and ideas, then organize them later.

2.      **Clarify the task in your own mind.** Visualize what the finished task or product should look like. Sometimes, leaders are disappointed with the work their people return to them because they themselves are not clear about what they wanted in the first place. Let your imaginations work. Anticipate.

**3.    Don't be a perfectionist.** If you receive a work that is not what you have in mind, discuss it, so that you can sort out the misunderstanding. If the work is acceptable, say, "This is fine for this time, but next time I'd like it done this way." Getting someone to redo acceptable work constantly to make it perfect is demoralizing, frustrating, and a waste of time. Again, set standards so that it would be easy to know what shall pass and what shall fail.

**4.    Do it right.** Choose planning tools that help you organize your meetings, appointments, tasks, projects, etc. in a consolidated manner. For example, find one form that serves more than one function, rather than having to deal with 6 different papers. If you're using something that doesn't help you feel organized, replace it with something that will.

**5.    Follow up.** Agree to check work in progress. If the person you have delegated to was given a week to complete a task, check with him in three days. Ask, "How are you doing on this project?" Rather than "Have you finished yet?" The latter puts him on the defensive end and increases pressure. You can catch potential problems in the task by checking up early.

## *WINNING QUALITY # 12: A Leader Should Be Able to Develop Other Leaders.*

You can only say that your organization is growing and leading towards the achievement of your goals when your people are growing. By growing, I mean being the next leaders that can help you carry the load...or carry a greater load in order to make things easier for all of you and make your success much nearer.

An effective leader can produce other leaders from his team. Otherwise, he is merely a guide that only directs his team towards somewhere he is not even sure of going, and nothing more. A good leader takes responsibilities, has strength of character, and is an effective communicator. He is an adviser, a mentor, a listener, and a friend all rolled into one. Who cannot develop better persons when you possess all these qualities?

Some leaders, as they call themselves, cannot develop other leaders usually because of their negative mentality. They see their people as hindrances for their personal success. They think, If I train my people to be better, they might turn out to be better than I am. These kinds of leader see leadership as competition instead of cooperation between them and their people. With this concept of leadership, it is no wonder why the team isn't growing and succeeding.

Either this or some leaders are just incapable of training their people to be potential leaders. In this case, you might want to assess yourself again if you are one effective leader. Those who are can train and develop other leaders.

Let me quote Peter Drucker as he said, "No executive has ever suffered because his people were strong and effective." Yes, there really is no harm in bringing out the best in your people. In fact, it is also you who benefits as you get brilliant minds to help you make decisions, organize the team, and develop more leaders...again.

Therefore, before you really consider yourself an effective leader and a winner, you should be able to impart your wisdom, share your skills and abilities, and mold people to be as effective and successful as you are, if not better.

## Bringing Out the Leader-Developer in You

Create an appropriate environment, nurture your people, and train them with the best knowledge and skills you know. Before you know it, there they are...your future successors! Remember what John Maxwell said, "There is no success without a successor." Here are some great methods to help your people develop their leadership potentials.

1.      **Be a good listener.** Good leaders are good listeners. They do not depend solely on their knowledge, but they give their people chances to express their viewpoints and they listen to them. Listening to your people adds success both to you and to their development. When you listen as they express their ideas and opinions, you actually are giving them a chance to contribute a solution, especially during problem solving and decision-making. Each time you hear out their ideas and give them credit, they will feel valued, and they will be encouraged to keep communicating with you. They will begin to develop greater judgment and understanding on serious matters.

2.      **Be concerned.** A great leader must be genuinely concerned with the well-being of his team. This concern shows itself by taking responsibility and defending his team if things do go wrong, by helping out those in difficulties, and by showing concern for those working extra hours.

Look out for them even outside the work. Although you do not have control over their personal lives, you must show concern for them about this aspect too. Things that seem to be of no importance to you might seem extremely critical to them. You must be able to empathize with them.

**3.     Learn to motivate.** Leaders can articulate their vision and ideals to others, convincing them of the value of their ideas. They can inspire people to work towards common goals and to achieve things they never thought they could do.

Learn how to motivate people. Explore the different needs that motivate people and recognize that the same rewards don't motivate everyone. Listen carefully to others to learn what motivates them.

However, do not confuse motivation with manipulation. Motivation occurs when you persuade others to take an action in their own best interests, while manipulation is persuading others to take an action that is primarily for your benefit. Leaders and motivators are winners; manipulators are losers who produce resentment and dispute. Become a motivator, lead your people, and never manipulate them.

**4.     Help others succeed.** Leaders empower others and go out of their way to help others achieve their full potential, thereby benefiting the organization. Give them a boost by mentoring individuals you feel are able to assume leadership roles. Share with them your knowledge and skills you know will help them become better individuals.

**5.     Challenge them!** Make their jobs challenging, exciting, and meaningful. Make them feel that they are individuals in a great team. People need meaningful work, even if it is tiring and unpleasant. They need to know that it is important and necessary for the survival of the organization. Some employees or workers who are given complicated jobs feel flattered and valued, thinking you trust them to do such challenging tasks.

**6.     Reward good behavior.** Although a certificate, letter, or a thank you may seem small, they can be powerful motivators. The reward should be specific and prompt. Do not say, "...for doing a good job." Cite the specific action that made you believe it was a good job. In addition, give guidance and assistance to your people when they need it. We all make mistakes and need help to achieve a particular goal.

## *CONCLUSION*

Being a leader sure is tough...lots of work, lots of responsibilities, lots of expectations. But even if you are capable to do all the work, take all the responsibilities, and reach all others' expectations, you still can never be a true leader unless you possess the 12 winning leadership qualities.

### A leader should have a vision and be able to cast it...

...He knows where to go and how to lead his team to be able to get there. A leader without a vision is like traveling in circles and getting lost just about every turn.

### A leader should be willing to take responsibilities...

...With great power as strong as leadership come great responsibilities. He who knows how to accept them shall be able to work on them. Only those who know how to work on them are real leaders.

### A leader should have strength of character...

...All effective leaders are winners. To be able to win, one needs good character such as perseverance, determination, patience, and confidence that would bring him to the top no matter how steep or rough the road is.

### A leader should have effective communication skills...

...He knows when to talk and when to listen. He is able to read even non-verbal signals from his people. He inspires, motivates, and moves them with his words.

### A leader should have a positive attitude...

...It is such attitude and thinking that would push him to go forward when all else is moving backwards. He makes things happen; especially those that others believe cannot push through.

### A leader should be influential...

...He can make his people work because they want to and not because they need to. He need not tell them what to do, but his vision and actions are already enough to let them know what to accomplish next.

## A leader should be disciplined...

...It is not because society expects him to be disciplined, but because he knows it is this character that could help him become a better person in mind, in heart, and in spirit.

## A leader should know how to develop trust...

...Trust is an important factor in making any relationship last. A leader should know how to trust his people and build trust from them.

## A leader should be willing to make changes...

...Otherwise, he is no more than any other follower is. He knows when and how to break the rules when necessary.

## A leader should know how and what to prioritize...

...Among all the responsibilities given to him, he can identify which is the most important and which is of lesser relevance. He does not focus on things that are not related to goal-attainment and the team's success.

## A leader should know what has to be done next...

...He sees the big picture and does not just focus on the present situation of the team. He plans and works out the best strategies for him and his people.

## Finally, a leader should be able to develop other leaders...

...He can identify who among his group are excellent and then develops them into better performers. He shares his abilities and imparts his wisdom to mold more leaders that can help make this world one successful place to live in.

An effective leader is all these. He stands out among the rest. He is, indeed, a winner.

## *BONUS*

Get Related Materials

from Our Free Library

# Instant Access – Join Here

*Click or type into your browser:*

*http://livesensical.com/go/byob/*